# WHERE DID DINOSAURS GO?

KU-033-272

Mike Unwin

Designed by Ian McNee
Illustrated by Andrew Robinson, Toni Goffe and Guy Smith

Cover design by Russell Punter
Cover illustration by Christyan Fox
With thanks to Katarina Dragoslavić and Rosie Dickins

Edited by Cheryl Evans and revised by Philippa Wingate

Consultant: Dr Angela Milner (The Natural History Museum, London)

## CONTENTS

2 What were dinosaurs?
4 What's left of dinosaurs
6 Dinosaur origins
8 Shapes and sizes
10 Dinosaur life
12 Alongside dinosaurs
14 Why did they die?
16 Big changes
18 A sudden change
20 After dinosaurs
22 Today
23 Internet links
24 Index

# What were dinosaurs?

Dinosaurs were animals that lived millions of years ago, before there were any people. Today there are no dinosaurs left.

Dinosaur means "terrible lizard". People called them this because their skeletons looked like giant lizards' skeletons. Now scientists know dinosaurs were not lizards. This book explains what they really were.

*Stegosaurus* was a dinosaur that lived 150 million years ago.

## Giants

Most dinosaurs were much bigger than the lizards you can see today.

*Diplodocus* was one of the longest dinosaurs. It grew up to 2m (89ft) long. That's as long as a tennis court.

The Komodo Dragon is the longest lizard alive today. It grows up to 3m (10ft) long.

## No more dinosaurs

65 million years ago dinosaurs became extinct. This means they disappeared forever. Nobody is sure why this happened. But experts have many ideas about it, as you will discover in this book.

***Internet link*** *For a link to a website where you can find out the difference between dinosaurs and other ancient reptiles and try an online game, go to* ***www.usborne-quicklinks.com***

## A long time ago

The time before people began to write is called prehistory. It is split into three different parts called eras. This picture tells you a little about each one.

225 million years ago

Dinosaurs appeared here.

This arrow has colours to show different eras.

Dinosaurs disappeared here.

65 million years ago

## Palaeozoic Era

*Trilobites* were small creatures that lived in the sea during the Palaeozoic Era. This was before dinosaurs.

## Mesozoic Era

Dinosaurs lived during the Mesozoic Era. This era can be split up into three different periods. Here you can see a dinosaur from each period.

*Plateosaurus* lived during the Triassic Period.

*Allosaurus* lived during the Jurassic Period.

*Styracosaurus* lived during the Cretaceous Period.

Dinosaurs were prehistoric animals that lived on Earth or 154 million years. People have only been around for about the last three million years.

## Caenozoic Era

*Brontotherium* was a big animal that lived during the Caenozoic Era. This was after dinosaurs.

People have not been here for long compared to dinosaurs.

People appeared about three million years ago.

This book will tell you lots of things about dinosaurs. It will also help you to understand what might have happened to them.

# What's left of dinosaurs

Experts have learned about dinosaurs by studying fossils. Fossils are the remains of animals that died a long time ago and have been turned into stone. They are all that is left of the dinosaurs now.

## How fossils were made

When a dinosaur died, its soft parts soon rotted away. But its hard skeleton was left.

If the dinosaur was in a muddy place such as the bottom of a lake, the skeleton sank into the mud.

As more mud covered the skeleton, the bottom layers were squashed and hardened into rock.

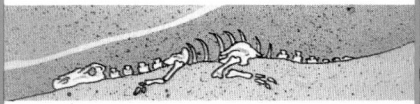

Over time, special minerals in the rock turned the skeleton to stone. This made it into a fossil.

## Dinosaur jigsaw puzzle

Scientists who study fossils are called palaeontologists. They fit the fossil pieces of a dinosaur together to find out what it looked like and how it lived.

This rock is 150 million years old.

A special hammer is used to chip rock from around the bones.

Palaeontologists photograph each fossil before they remove it, so they know exactly where it was found.

Fossils are found in places that were once covered by water. Here you can see a dinosaur fossil being dug out of a cliff.



***Internet link*** *For a link to a website with a slideshow that follows a dinosaur fossil from its discovery to its display in a museum, go to* ***www.usborne-quicklinks.com***

## Getting it wrong

Palaeontologists can make mistakes. When scientists first put *Iguanodon* together, they found a bone that did not seem to fit the rest of the skeleton. They decided that it belonged on *Iguanodon's* nose, like a rhinoceros's horn. But when they found more fossils they realized that this bone was a spike on *Iguanodon*'s thumb.

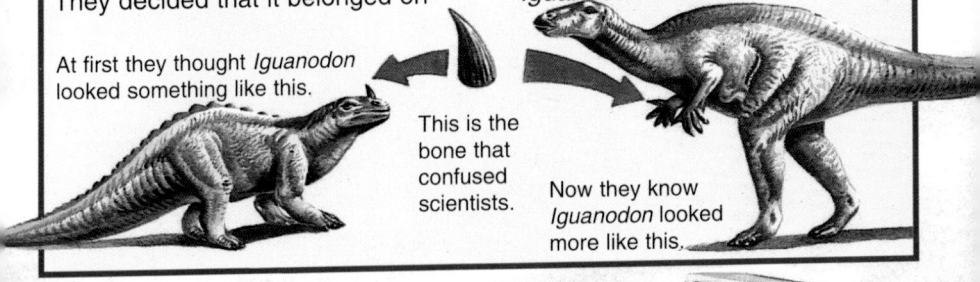


Experts wrap fossils in damp paper and plaster to protect them. Each one is given a number.

Fossils are packed and taken away to be studied.

## More to come

In 1965, palaeontologists in Mongolia found the huge arms of a dinosaur called *Deinocheirus.* They are still looking for its body.

*Deinocheirus's* arms were longer than a man.

# Dinosaur origins

It helps to understand why dinosaurs disappeared if you know where they came from. Most scientists think all living things gradually change. This change is called evolution.

Your environment is the area where you live. Evolution makes animals change, or evolve, to suit their environment.

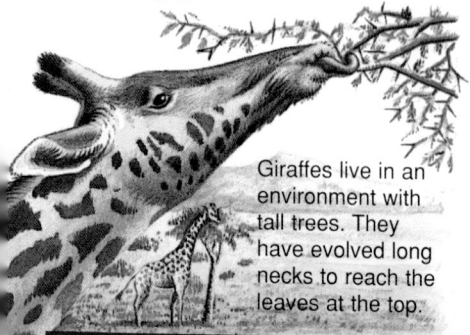

Giraffes live in an environment with tall trees. They have evolved long necks to reach the leaves at the top.

## From water to land

Here you can see how dinosaurs evolved over millions of years.

Over 350 million years ago, no animals lived on the land. But where pools began to dry up, some fish began to leave the water.

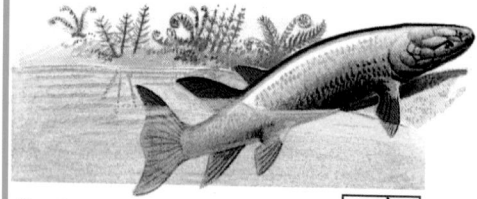

*Eusthenopteron* was a fish that used its strong fins like legs.

## How to survive

Sometimes environments can change. Animals that are suited to the changes survive, but others die. A famous scientist, Charles Darwin, called this natural selection.

Not everybody believes in evolution and natural selection. Many people believe God created Earth and put animals on it as they are now.

 ***Internet link*** *For a link to a website where you can find out more about evolution and natural selection with an online experiment, go to* ***www.usborne-quicklinks.com***

350 million years ago, animals with legs, called amphibians, evolved. They lived on land, but they had to be close to water to lay eggs.

*Ichthyostega* was an amphibian. Its legs carried it low over the ground.

*Dimetrodon* was a reptile. Its legs stuck out from the sides of its body.

310 million years ago, animals called reptiles evolved. Their bodies were now suited to life on the land. They had dry, scaly skin to protect them from the sun.

*Diplodocus* had pillar-like legs.

230 million years ago, some reptiles evolved stronger and straighter legs. These were the first dinosaurs.

## Natural selection at work

Peppered moths show how a changing environment can make animals evolve.

**1.** Some Peppered moths are dark and some are pale. 200 years ago there were more pale moths.

**2.** Pale moths were the same shade as trees, so birds caught more dark ones, which were easier to see.

**3.** When factories were built, smoke made the trees darker. Birds now found it easier to catch pale moths.

**4.** More dark moths survived and had dark babies. Dark moths soon became more common.

# Shapes and sizes

Dinosaurs evolved into many different sizes. Some were quite small. Others were much bigger than any land animals alive today.

*Brachiosaurus* was one of the biggest dinosaurs. It could weigh more than 50 tonnes (51 tons). That's the same as nine elephants.

*Brachiosaurus*' back bones were light but very strong to help carry its heavy body.

Strong legs supported its weight.

## Keeping warm

Animals cannot survive if they get too hot or too cold. A dinosaur's temperature changed with the heat of the sun. In cool weather, dinosaurs got cold.

The biggest dinosaurs were so huge that it took them a very long time to cool down. So their great size helped them to keep warm.

## Using a sail

*Spinosaurus* had a special sail on its back to keep its body at the right temperature. As the sun moved, *Spinosaurus* changed position.

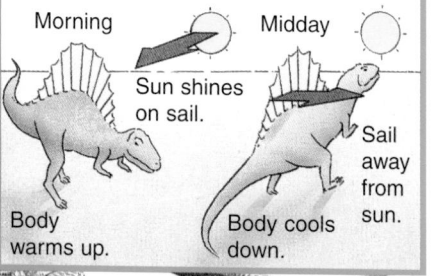

## Different shapes

Dinosaurs evolved into different shapes for different reasons.

Ceratopians had huge heads with bony frills and sharp horns. *Triceratops* was the biggest ceratopian. It was 11m (36ft) long and weighed 5.4 tonnes (6 tons).

*Parasaurolophus* called to others by making loud trumpeting noises through its crest.

*Parasaurolophus* had a bony beak for tearing off plants to eat, and a bony crest on its head.

*Triceratops* had sharp horns to keep enemies away.

A bony frill protected its neck and held strong muscles for working its jaws.

*Euoplocephalus* was a heavy dinosaur covered in bony plates and spikes for protection.

*Euoplocephalus* used its tail as a club to defend itself.

## Make a dinosaur

You could make a *Euoplocephalus* with balls of clay, used matches and thumb tacks.

Roll a big ball for the body.

Roll smaller balls for the head, legs and club.

Roll a sausage shape for the tail.

Use broken matches for the spikes.

Use thumb tacks for the bony plates.

# Dinosaur life

Fossil clues help experts to find out how dinosaurs lived. This also helps them to discover what changes may have made dinosaurs die out.

## Clues about food

Some dinosaurs had sharp teeth and strong claws. This shows that they ate meat. *Tyrannosaurus* was one of the biggest meat-eaters. It was as heavy as an elephant and as long as a bus.

### How you eat

People can eat many different kinds of food. You have different teeth for different jobs. Look at your mouth in a mirror and feel inside with clean fingers.

Can you feel sharp front teeth for cutting and flat back teeth for grinding?

Other dinosaurs had special teeth for eating plants. *Corythosaurus* was a plant-eater. It chewed on tough leaves and twigs.

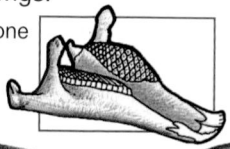

*Corythosaurus's* jawbone shows hundreds of small teeth for grinding plants.

*Tyrannosaurus* had sharp teeth for cutting meat.

It had strong claws for tearing open its prey.

*Corythosaurus*

Fossil dinosaur droppings can show what dinosaurs ate.

Pine needles in dropping.

## Eggs

Scientists know that some dinosaurs laid eggs, because they have found lots of fossil ones. The biggest eggs are over 30cm (1ft) across.

Baby *Protoceratops* hatched from eggs laid in the sand to keep them warm.

## Staying together

Lots of fossil *Triceratops* have been found together. This shows that they probably lived in herds.

Experts think adult *Triceratops* surrounded their babies to protect them from danger.

## Fossil footprints

*Velociraptor* was a fierce hunter. It was only 2m (6½ft) long, but its fossil footprints are spaced far apart. This shows how fast *Velociraptor* could run.

*Velociraptor's* long, stiff tail helped it to balance when it was running or jumping.

Long legs helped it to take big strides.

## Fighting

Some dinosaurs that lived in herds fought each other to decide upon a leader. The thick skull bone of the male *Pachycephalosaurus* was probably used to protect it in fights.

*Pachycephalosaurus* fought with their heads, like goats do.

# Alongside dinosaurs

While dinosaurs were living on the land, other prehistoric reptiles were living in the sea and the air. Interestingly, they disappeared at exactly the same time as dinosaurs.

## Sea monsters

Huge reptiles lived in the sea. Their long, smooth bodies made them good swimmers. Their legs evolved into flippers to help them swim.

Ichthyosaurs grew up to 12m (38ft) long. They did not lay eggs, but gave birth to their young underwater.

Plesiosaurs grew up to 12m (38ft) long. They came onto land to lay their eggs.

Ichthyosaurs could leap like dolphins.

Sharp teeth for catching fish

Big eyes for seeing underwater

Ichthyosaurs had hand bones inside their flippers. This shows they were reptiles and not fish.

## In the air

Pterosaurs were flying reptiles. They had wings made of skin, just like bats today. They also had very light bones to help them fly. Some were no bigger than a sparrow. Others were the size of a small aircraft.

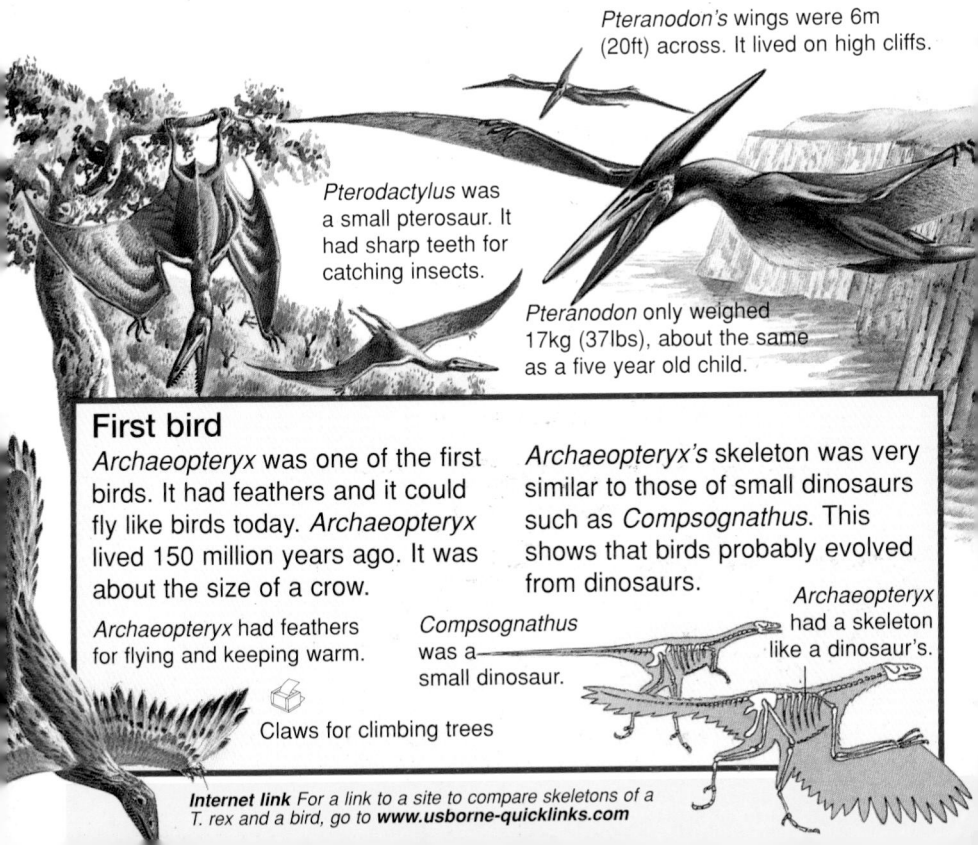


### First bird

*Archaeopteryx* was one of the first birds. It had feathers and it could fly like birds today. *Archaeopteryx* lived 150 million years ago. It was about the size of a crow.

*Archaeopteryx's* skeleton was very similar to those of small dinosaurs such as *Compsognathus*. This shows that birds probably evolved from dinosaurs.

***Internet link*** *For a link to a site to compare skeletons of a T. rex and a bird, go to* ***www.usborne-quicklinks.com***

# Why did they die?

Experts know when dinosaurs died out, but they are still not sure why. There are different ideas about what might have happened. Now scientists know many of these ideas are wrong.

## Finding out from rocks

Fossil dinosaurs are found in rocks from the Mesozoic Era. But there are none in rocks that are newer than this.

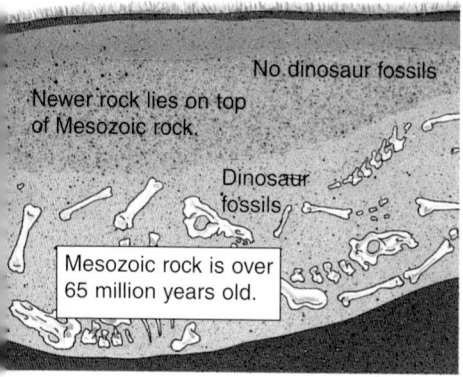


This shows that dinosaurs all became extinct 65 million years ago, at the end of the Mesozoic Era.

## Too big?

Some scientists thought dinosaurs grew so huge that they could not support their own weight.

Now experts know that big dinosaurs had very strong skeletons.

Small dinosaurs became extinct too. So size can not explain why they all died out.

## Dying of diseases?

Some scientists thought diseases made dinosaurs extinct.

Some dinosaurs had diseases, but they evolved to survive these. Now experts know that disease on its own can never make a type of animal extinct.

## Beaten by mammals?

During the Mesozoic Era, a new kind of creature called mammals evolved. (You can read more about them later.)

Some experts thought mammals ate all the dinosaurs' food.

Others thought mammals stole dinosaurs' eggs.

Now scientists are sure that mammals did not make dinosaurs extinct. Mammals only became important after dinosaurs died out.

## Poisonous flowers?

The first flowering plants evolved during the Cretaceous Period. Some experts thought they had chemicals that poisoned dinosaurs.

Now scientists know that new kinds of dinosaurs evolved especially to eat the new plants.

## End of the line

During the Mesozoic Era, new dinosaurs always evolved to take the place of others. But at the end of the Era, dinosaurs all died out together, and no more evolved to replace them.

Something must have happened that killed all the dinosaurs and stopped new ones from evolving. The next four pages tell you more about this.

# Big changes

The environment changed in many different ways while dinosaurs lived on Earth. Scientists think this might explain why dinosaurs died out.

## Changes in plants

Many different kinds of plants evolved during the Mesozoic Era.

These plants lived during the Triassic and Jurassic Periods.

Horsetails

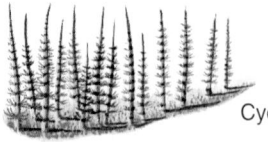

Cycads

These plants lived during the Cretaceous Period.

Hardwood trees

Flowering plants

Changes in plants meant dinosaurs' food was always changing too. But these changes were so gradual that dinosaurs could evolve to keep up.

## Changes in the weather

The climate is the kind of weather that any place usually has.

Earth had a warm climate for most of the Mesozoic Era.

But at the end of the Cretaceous Period it became cooler. Experts think that cold weather helped to make dinosaurs extinct.

Most dinosaurs had no fur or feathers to help store their body heat. Most of them were too big to warm up again after a long, cold winter.

## Changes in the Earth's surface

The Earth's surface is broken into large pieces called plates. These move around so that continents are always slowly changing position. This is called continental drift.

As the plates move, the Earth's environment and climate change. Some experts think this made dinosaurs extinct. These maps show how the Earth has changed.

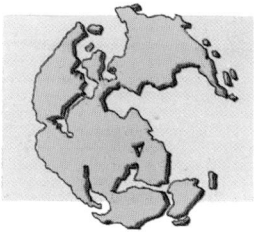

During the Triassic Period, there was just one big continent called Pangaea. The climate was warm all around the world.

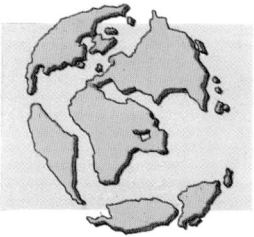

During the Cretaceous Period, Pangaea split up into new continents and oceans were left in between them. Earth's climate became cooler.

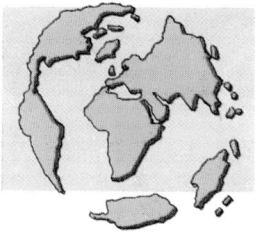

This is what the Earth looks like today. The continents are still moving, but it happens too slowly for you to tell.

### In the sea

As the land changed, so did the sea. Some experts think this killed millions of tiny sea creatures called *Foraminifera*, and other animals that ate them.

*Foraminifera* and many other sea creatures died out with dinosaurs.

### Too slow

Continental drift takes a very long time. On its own, it does not explain why dinosaurs and other creatures all died out so suddenly.

# A sudden change

Now scientists think dinosaurs died out because something violent suddenly changed the Earth's climate. Here is what may have happened.

## Nothing left to eat

All living things in any environment depend upon each other for their food. This is called a food web.

If the dinosaurs' food web broke at the end of the Mesozoic Era, they would have died out. Here you can see why.

No plants

Plant-eaters died.

Meat-eaters died.

## What broke the food web?

Many scientists think a big lump of rock from outer space, called an asteroid, struck the Earth at the end of the Mesozoic Era.

The asteroid was probably 10 to 15km (6 to 9 miles) across.

## Where it landed

There are clues that an asteroid hit what is now Yucatan in Mexico.

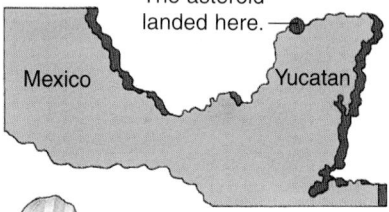

Experts have found tiny glass beads like this around the area. They are made of rock that melted when the asteroid struck the Earth.

## No sunlight

All living things close to where the asteroid struck were killed. Dust and gases filled the air around the world. Sunlight was blocked out and the world became cold and dark.

Without sunlight, all the plants died.

When plants died, the food web broke down. This killed dinosaurs, and they soon became extinct.

## How plants grow

You can see how plants need sunlight. Put some damp paper towel on a saucer and scatter cress seeds on it.

Leave the saucer in sunlight so the seeds can grow

Cover some shoots.

Take the cover off after a week. The shoots without any sunlight will have died.

## Volcanoes

65 million years ago there were also some huge volcanic eruptions in what is now India. These might have caused as much damage as an asteroid.

Some experts think dust and gases from these volcanoes might have blocked out the sunlight too.

## Too hot?

When the asteroid struck, it threw up water droplets as well as dust. After the dust settled, water droplets stayed in the air. It trapped the heat of the sun, so the Earth heated up like a giant greenhouse.

Just as dinosaurs would have been killed by cold, they also would have died if it was too hot.

# After dinosaurs

Not everything became extinct at the end of the Mesozoic Era. Plants grew up from seeds that had survived, and soon other animals began to fill the places left by dinosaurs.

More birds evolved to live in the air.

Some reptiles, such as crocodiles and turtles, still lived in fresh water.

Small mammals lived in the trees and forests.

## About mammals

Mammals are animals that can keep their bodies warm all the time. Most mammals have fur or hair and do not lay eggs. They give birth to babies and feed them on milk.

*Purgatorius* lived 70 million years ago when dinosaurs were still around. It probably slept during the day, and came out at night. All later mammals evolved from animals like this.

*Purgatorius* was the size of a rat. It ate insects, and came out at night when dinosaurs were asleep.

## Staying alive

Mammals' warm bodies helped them to survive when the climate changed. They were also small enough to burrow holes and escape from the cold or heat.

## Different kinds of mammal

The time since dinosaurs died out is called the Caenozoic Era. Many different mammals have evolved and died out during this time. Here you can see some that are now extinct.

*Paraceratherium* was the largest ever land mammal. It was 8m (26ft) tall, six times as high as a man.

*Eohippus* was one of the first horses. It was only the size of a fox.

Sabre-toothed cats were fierce hunters, just like tigers today.

### Out of the trees

People are mammals. Most experts think we evolved from creatures like apes that lived in the trees about 10 million years ago.

The first people were hunters who could walk upright on two legs. They learned how to use tools, build shelters and make fire.

## Dinosaur relatives

Tuataras lived over 150 million years ago, at the same time as dinosaurs. Some still live in New Zealand today.

Tuatara

Chaffinch

Modern birds evolved from prehistoric birds like *Archaeopteryx*, and they still have very similar skeletons to dinosaurs. This shows that birds are dinosaurs' closest relatives today.

# Today

Since dinosaurs died out, many other living things have become extinct. Today most extinctions are caused by the things people do.

## Damage to wildlife

Wildlife means all the wild plants and animals living in the world. The main danger to wildlife comes from people damaging or changing the environment where it lives.

On the island of Madagascar people have chopped down the forests where lemurs live. Now very few lemurs are left.

Pollution is waste, such as poisonous chemicals, left by people. Pollution in the environment harms everything that lives there.

Oil spilled in the sea kills many sea birds, such as cormorants.

## Hunting

If animals are hunted too much, they can become extinct. People usually hunt animals for food or for their skins.

Dodos were once hunted for food. They became extinct 300 years ago.

## Living together

It is important to protect wildlife. All living things are connected to each other by food webs. If one thing disappears, many others may suffer. For example, snakes eat rats. In parts of Africa, people killed lots of snakes. Soon there were too many rats. They ate people's crops, so people suffered.

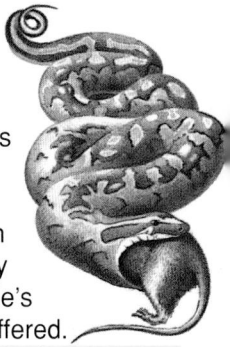

 ***Internet link*** *For a link to a website where you can find out more about dinosaurs and birds, with online activities, go to* ***www.usborne-quicklinks.com***

# Internet links

For links to more websites about dinosaurs, go to the Usborne Quicklinks Website at **www.usborne-quicklinks.com** and click on the number of the website you want to visit.

**Website 1** – Explore theories about why dinosaurs disappeared, with clickable facts and animations.

**Website 2** – Find out why dinosaur fossils are found in places where dinosaurs never lived.

**Website 3** – Find out how discoveries over the years have changed our view of dinosaurs.

**Website 4** – Watch amazing animations of dinosaurs and see how they lived, then have some fun with online games, ecards and lots of other dinosaur activities.

**Website 5** – Here you'll find information, games and quizzes about dinosaurs.

**Website 6** – Join in an egg hunt and see how scientists "hatch" fossilized eggs.

**Website 7** – Unearth the skeletons of six different dinosaurs in a virtual dig, with clickable facts, then print out a dinosaur word search.

**Website 8** – Explore the history of dinosaur science, and take a look at a fascinating gallery of famous scientific mistakes.

**Website 9** – Read a photo essay about how scientists put together the bones of a giant dinosaur.

**Website 10** – Find out about fossil collecting and how to make a fossil cast.

# Index

amphibian, 7
*Archaeopteryx*, 13, 21
asteroid, 18, 19

birds, 13, 20, 21
*Brachiosaurus*, 8

conservation, 22
continental drift, 17
*Corythosaurus*, 10

*Deinocheirus*, 5
*Dimetrodon*, 7
*Diplodocus*, 2,7
disease, 14
droppings, 10

eggs, 7, 11, 12
environment, 6, 16, 18, 22
Eras, 3
  Caenozoic, 3, 21
  Mesozoic, 3, 14, 15, 16, 18, 20
  Palaeozoic, 3
*Euoplocphalus*, 9
evolution, 6-7, 8-9, 12-13, 20-21
extinction, 2, 14-15, 16-17, 18-19, 22

fighting, 11
fish, 6, 12
flying, 13
food, 10
food web, 18, 22
footprints, 11
fossils, 4-5, 10-11, 14

hunting, 22

Ichthyosaur, 12
*Icthyostega*, 7
*Iguanodon*, 5

lizards, 2

mammals, 15, 20-21
meat-eaters, 10, 18

*Pachycephalosaurus*, 11
palaeontologists, 4-5
Pangaea, 17
*Parasaurolophus*, 9
Peppered Moth, 7
Period, 3
  Cretaceous, 3, 15, 16-17
  Jurassic, 3, 16
  Triassic, 3, 16, 17

plant-eaters, 10, 18
plant, 10, 15, 16, 22
Pleiosaurs, 12
pollution, 22
*Protoceratops*, 11
Pterosaurs, 13

reptiles, 7
rocks, 4, 14

sea, 13, 17
skeleton, 2, 4-5, 13
*Spinosaurus*, 8
*Stegosaurus*, 2
sunlight, 8, 19

temperature, 8, 16-17, 19, 20
*Triceratops*, 9, 11
*Tuatara*, 21
*Tyrannosaurus*, 10

*Velociraptor*, 11
volcanoes, 19

weather, 8, 16, 19, 20
wildlife, 20-21

Usborne Publishing are not responsible, and do not accept liability, for the availability or content of any Web site other than our own, or for any exposure to harmful, offensive or inaccurate material which may appear on the Web. Usborne Publishing will have no liability for any damage or loss caused by viruses that may be downloaded as a result of browsing the sites we recommend.
Usborne downloadable pictures are the copyright of Usborne Publishing Ltd and may not be reproduced in print or in electronic form for any commercial or profit-related purpose.

First published in 2001 by Usborne Publishing Ltd., Usborne House, 83-85 Saffron Hill, London EC1N 8RT, England. **www.usborne.com**
First published in America in 2002. UE
Copyright © 2001, 1991 Usborne Publishing Ltd. The name Usborne and the devices are Trade Marks of Usborne Publishing Ltd. All rights reserved. No part of this publication may be reproduced, stored in a retrieval system, or transmitted in any form or by any means, electronic, mechanical, photocopying, recording, or otherwise, without the prior permission of the publisher. Printed in China.